Ocean Liners
Crossing and Cruising the Seven Seas

Karl Zimmermann
Photography by the author

BOYDS MILLS PRESS
HONESDALE, PENNSYLVANIA

Acknowledgments

Theodore W. Scull, a longtime friend and a preeminent expert on ships both past and present, kindly reviewed this book's manuscript. For this I'm most grateful. Any errors that may have found their way onto these pages are, of course, mine alone. Thanks also to Ben Lyons, currently first officer on the *Queen Mary 2*, for patiently answering numerous technical questions.

Right from the beginning I've found Larry Rosler, the editorial director at Boyds Mills Press, and Tim Gillner, the art director, to be consummate professionals. Now that we've collaborated on four books, I consider them good friends as well.

From that day in August 1967 when we set sail together aboard the *Bremen*, my wife, Laurel, has been with me on virtually every sea voyage I've made. Her support and keen editorial eye are always invaluable, and her companionship makes it all worthwhile.

The photographs in the book are mine or from my collection, except:

pp. 12–13. Painting by John Wilson, courtesy of SS Great Britain Trust.

p. 14, courtesy of Cunard Line.

pp. 15 and 16, courtesy of SS Great Britain Trust.

p. 17 bottom, courtesy of Library of Congress.

p. 26 left, courtesy of Library of Congress.

I'm grateful for permission to include these images in the book.

—K.Z.

Text and photographs copyright © 2008 by Karl Zimmermann
All rights reserved

Boyds Mills Press, Inc.
815 Church Street
Honesdale, Pennsylvania 18431
Printed in China

Library of Congress Cataloging-in-Publication Data

Zimmermann, Karl R.
    Ocean liners : crossing and cruising the seven seas / Karl Zimmermann. — 1st ed.
        p. cm.
    ISBN 978-1-59078-552-2 (hardcover : alk. paper)
    1. Ocean liners—Juvenile literature. 2. Ocean travel—Juvenile literature. I. Title.

VM381.Z56 2008
387.2'432—dc22
                                        2007049323

First edition
The text of this book is set in 13-point Minion.

10 9 8 7 6 5 4 3 2 1

From my father I inherited a love of ocean liners. This book is dedicated to his memory.

Jacket and cover: *Royal Caribbean's* Adventure of the Seas
Title page: *Historic fireboat* John J. Harvey *extends a traditional welcome to the* Queen Mary 2 *on its maiden arrival into New York City.*

Contents

Introduction

A Gift of
Ocean Liners

THE GREAT SHIPS THAT SAIL THE OCEANS ARE THE LARGEST objects in the world that move—huge, majestic creatures that demand our attention. And among ships, the glamorous passenger-carrying ocean liners have always been the grandest of all. In their heyday they sailed all over the world, but the route across the Atlantic Ocean between Europe and North America was always the busiest—and most competitive. This route became known as the "Atlantic Ferry" because its ships were so numerous and their crossings so frequent.

Liners, particularly those sailing the North Atlantic, once carried millions of immigrants who traveled in overcrowded conditions, and they also coddled the wealthy in exquisite staterooms. Jet airplanes have almost completely replaced the liners that crossed the Atlantic. Scheduled trips, such as those across the Atlantic, are called "line voyages," which is the origin of the term "liner."

◄ *In cruise service, Chandris Line's* Amerikanis *steams into New York Harbor, passing the Statue of Liberty. The ship was built in 1951 as* Kenya Castle *for line voyages between England and Africa.*

As a small boy, I sailed with my parents aboard the Ile de France *(top photo) and the* Nieuw Amsterdam *(bottom photos).*

The Queen Elizabeth 2 *steams up the Hudson River to its berth in Manhattan.*

Still, passenger shipping is booming today. Travelers can board a growing fleet of "cruise" ships to tour every corner of the world just for fun. Most often they return to the port where they started. Many of these new ships are huge, carrying well over two thousand, three thousand, or even four thousand pleasure-seeking passengers. Sometimes I'm among them.

Growing up near New York City, I was given a gift a long time ago that I didn't fully appreciate until many years later. That gift was ocean liners, the graceful ships that sped (or sometimes plodded) across the Atlantic and the world's other oceans.

Part of the gift was simply the presence of these great ships, which I could see whenever I drove to New York City with my family. From New Jersey we'd cross the George Washington Bridge. Then, riding south along the Hudson River, I'd eagerly scan the distant piers for "funnels," as ships' smokestacks are called. By their color, size, number, and arrangement, I often could identify the ships docked at the city's impressive row of "finger piers" that reached out into the harbor like an unclenched fist. I might see the banded black-and-red funnels, each different, of the Cunard Line, the French Line, or the United States Lines. North German Lloyd's funnels were mustard-colored, and Holland America Line's were yellow with green and white bands.

Getting Aboard the Liners

But an even better part of the gift was the chance to sail to and from Europe on these liners. Just living for a week or more in what seemed like a city in motion was great fun. Standing at the rail, I was mesmerized by the wash of the ocean against the hull as the ship sliced through the water, and there was always the chance of spotting a whale.

I reveled in the rituals of life at sea: the meals, served in high style by the dining-room stewards; the deck sports, like shuffleboard and Ping-Pong; the daily attempt to guess the mileage traveled since the previous noon. Even today I remember those great liners on which I sailed—the *Ile de France*, the *Nieuw Amsterdam*, the *Mauretania*, the *Bremen*.

But the first commercial jet crossed the Atlantic in 1958, and quickly sea travel to Europe began to disappear. People were

Ships have a special majesty at night. Launched in 1965, the Sagafjord *was among the last liners built for transatlantic service.*

With the help of Moran tugboats, the Amerikanis *and* Queen Elizabeth 2 *dock in New York City. Moran tugs have long been a familiar sight up and down the East Coast of the United States. Modern cruise ships typically don't require tugs for docking, since they're usually equipped with "thrusters"—lateral propellers within the hull that can move a ship's bow or stern sideways.*

simply in too much of a hurry to spend a week sailing across the Atlantic when they could make the trip by air in less than half a day. Through the decade of the 1970s, the once-booming "Atlantic Ferry" vanished ship by ship. By that time, however, "cruising"—traveling by ship for recreation, not transportation—had begun to gain popularity. Cruising has grown ever since. At first cruise ships were mostly the old liners finding a new role, but during the 1990s most of these old-timers were replaced by much bigger ships that offer onboard activities that no one could have imagined twenty years ago. Today, some ships have climbing walls. One has a planetarium, and another a skating rink.

Remembering Old Friends

Ships have personalities, so passengers naturally develop their favorites, which they regret losing. I remember waking up many years ago to a radio broadcast reporting that the *Hanseatic*, on which I'd recently sailed, was burning at its pier in

With midtown Manhattan as a backdrop, the Regal Empress *backs into the Hudson. The ship was built in 1953 as the Greek Line's* Olympia *for transatlantic service. A Princess Cruises vessel has just finished "bunkering"—taking on fuel—at the pier.*

New York. All of my other early ships are now long gone as well. Some were cut up by scrappers once they became obsolete—or simply wore out from age.

Now most of the "finger piers" reaching out into the Hudson River are gone, but cruise ships continue to sail from the Port of New York. Some now use new terminals in Brooklyn's Red Hook section or Bayonne in New Jersey, but others still dock at the New York Cruise Terminal in Manhattan. So even now, as I drive along the Hudson River, I study the placement and marking of ships' funnels, still pleased to be able to identify the vessels and the lines that operate them.

In the twenty-first century, most sea voyagers cruise aboard such giant ships as the Serenade of the Seas *(above).*

Open decks invite cool breezes and provide a place to gaze at the sea.

One

From Sail to Steam

Dᴜʀɪɴɢ ᴛʜᴇ ɴɪɴᴇᴛᴇᴇɴᴛʜ ᴄᴇɴᴛᴜʀʏ, ꜱᴛᴇᴀᴍ ᴘᴏᴡᴇʀ revolutionized transportation. On land, it replaced horses and mules pulling carriages and wagons and canal boats. At sea, it replaced sails. For a time ships carried both sails and steam engines, but before long steam took over and remained in charge for nearly a century, until it in turn was replaced by diesel and diesel-electric propulsion.

Though passenger ships had been sailing the seas for centuries, the era of the ocean liner properly begins with the introduction of steam. This brought speed and, even more important, far greater reliability. Wind was unpredictable, making fixed schedules impossible.

Although he invented none of its key components, Isambard Kingdom Brunel deserves recognition as the father of the ocean liner. His first ship, the *Great Western*, was narrowly beaten in 1838 by the competing *Sirius* in a race to complete the first crossing of the Atlantic made primarily with steam propulsion. (Both ships were wooden-hulled paddle-wheel steamers.) However, the *Great Western* actually made the crossing in less time (the *Sirius* had a head start) and immediately began regular transatlantic service, becoming the first steamship to do so.

◀ *Isambard Kingdom Brunel's* Great Britain *as it appeared in 1852, with extra sail added for immigrant service to Australia.*

Samuel Cunard's paddle-wheel steamer Britannia.

The *Great Western*'s crossings typically took about fourteen days. Even with optimum winds and the most skilled captain, sailing ships typically took twenty-two days or more. Even though the *Great Western* was important, Brunel's second ship, the steel-hulled, propeller-driven *Great Britain*, launched in 1843, is considered the first great ocean liner.

Not long after the *Great Western* entered service, Samuel Cunard, a Canadian, was awarded a contract to carry the mail between England and his native Halifax, in Nova Scotia. His first ship, the *Britannia*, was launched in 1840. It was followed immediately by three similar ships, since four vessels were needed to offer frequent, reliable mail service. These four were wooden-hulled, sidewheel-equipped, sail-assisted steamships, similar to the *Great Western* in size and speed.

Cunard's steamship company flourished and grew. In fact, the British-based Cunard Line is very much alive today. Its *Queen Mary 2* is the sole ship regularly crossing the Atlantic Ocean. Its newest vessel, the *Queen Victoria*, was launched in December 2007.

As steam-assisted sail power gave way to sail-assisted steam power, sail-carrying masts became smaller and fewer, eventually disappearing altogether. While this was happening, more and more lines entered the competition for trade across the North Atlantic and the world's other oceans. Most European countries with access to the sea—France, Germany, Holland, Belgium, Sweden, Norway, Italy, Greece, Denmark, Poland, and Spain, along with Great Britain—eventually participated. So did the United States and Canada.

Like Cunard, Holland America Line is an early company still active in today's cruise business. Its first ship, the *Rotterdam*, entered the transatlantic trade in 1872 and took fifteen days to make the crossing from Rotterdam to New York. (All the line's passenger ships were, and still are, given names that end in "dam.") By this time, two German lines were operating, Hamburg-Amerika and North German Lloyd, as was the Compagnie Générale Transatlantique, called the French Line. So too was the White Star Line, the British competitor to Cunard that became best known as the operator of the famous and tragic *Titanic*.

White Star's *Oceanic* of 1872 marked another significant step in liner development. It introduced bathtubs and running water and the "promenade deck," a space where passengers could walk and enjoy the fresh air. As the years passed, ships grew larger and more comfortable, accumulating the plush features that first-class and even second-class "cabin" passengers (those who had private rooms) would come to expect in the golden age of sea travel, which was close at hand. Staterooms became spacious and luxurious. Lounges resembled those in the finest hotels. Meals were extensive and exquisite.

Brunel and the Great Britain

Born in 1806, Isambard Kingdom Brunel was a remarkable man with a distinctive name. A multitalented engineer, he is perhaps best known as the builder of the Great Western Railway from London to Bristol, an English seaport. In fact, his Great Western Steamship Company was created as an overseas extension of the railway. Brunel also designed some important bridges and railway stations.

The *Great Britain*, Brunel's second ship, was daring in a number of ways. It was the first iron-hulled, propeller-driven liner. With a length of 322 feet, it was the largest ship of its time. Iron "bulkheads," or walls, separated the hull into five watertight compartments As future liners would, it offered fine accommodations for first-class passengers and Spartan ones for immigrants traveling in "steerage."

The *Great Britain*'s life as a pioneering transatlantic liner was brief, ending when it ran aground after just a few successful crossings. Sold by financially troubled Great Western Steamship, it then carried immigrants from England to Australia for more than twenty years. For this service, its 1,000-horsepower engine (at the time, the largest marine engine ever made) was replaced by a smaller one and additional sails were installed. Thus, for economy of operation, the Great Britain was changed from a "sail-assist steamship" to steam-assisted sail.

Next, steam was abandoned altogether, and the *Great Britain* became a sail-only ship called a "windjammer," a term applied to large iron- or steel-hulled sail-powered cargo vessels. After it was damaged by the wild seas of Cape Horn at the southern tip of South America, the ship found refuge in the nearby Falkland Islands, its sailing days over. It served there for nearly half a century as a warehouse for coal or wool. In 1937, it was taken to shallow offshore waters and "scuttled"— intentionally sunk.

Brunel stands in front of chains used to restrain ships at their launchings.

The Great Britain *is moored in Bristol in 1844, the year after it was launched there.*

The ship's next life has been perhaps its most remarkable. In 1970, the ship was refloated, then transported back to Bristol on pontoons. Today, it sits in the dry dock where it was built, magnificently restored as a museum.

Brunel would build one more ship, the hulking *Great Eastern* of 1859, a giant well more than twice the length of the *Great Britain*. Powered with paddle wheels and designed for service between Great Britain and India and Australia, the vessel could carry four thousand passengers. Never a success in that role, the *Great Eastern* finally came into its own laying telephone cables across the oceans. Shortly after the ship's launching, Brunel died of a stroke at age fifty-three, a death possibly hastened by troubles with the ship.

No bigger ship was built until White Star Line's *Celtic* in 1901, forty-two years later.

The SS Baltic *(left) was built in 1904 for the White Star Line, which later would own the ill-fated* Titanic.

For steerage passengers (below), life on board was anything but luxurious.

Immigrants Fill the Ships

Most of the passengers on ships were immigrants, bound for a new life in the United States or Canada or Australia or elsewhere. They traveled in "steerage," where conditions were extremely primitive but fares were affordable. Since it cost little to carry them, these passengers were the greatest source of income for the shipping companies in the liners' early years.

Imagine the everyday heroism of these immigrants, who left their homes, often their families, and most of their possessions behind to go to a strange land where many could speak only a few words of the native language. The Irish were among the first to leave, in the 1840s, because of the "Potato Famine." The massive failure of that essential crop in Ireland left a million dead and sent a like number fleeing to North America. Germans came, and Scandinavians and Eastern Europeans and Russians and Italians. Unlike today's cruise-ship passengers, they hoped and prayed for the voyage to end as quickly and painlessly as possible.

Steerage passengers were confined to a space deep in the hull—often at the aft (rear) end. The steering gear was also there,

hence the name. In an open dormitory, steerage passengers would sleep in bunks, typically three-tiered. They may have been supplied with blankets but usually not pillows. Meals were simple and repetitious, served at long communal tables. The accommodations were cramped, claustrophobic, bad-smelling, and lacking in fresh air and light. If the seas were rough, waves slammed against the

hull, making steerage passengers feel as if they were being shaken inside a drum. They were restricted to a small sliver of the least attractive open deck space. In contrast, first class was in the choicest location: high up, for light and air, and at the center of the ship, where motion was least noticeable.

But steerage passage was the lines' bread and butter. Brunel's *Great Eastern* was designed to carry 596 cabin passengers and 2,400 in steerage. Holland America Line's *Statendam*, launched in 1898, carried 200 first-class passengers, 175 second-class, and 1,000 in steerage. Cunard Line's *Carpathia*, launched in 1902, carried 204 first-class passengers and 1,500 in steerage. Hamburg-Amerika Line's *Amerika*, launched in 1905, carried 420 first-class passengers, 254 second-class, 223 third-class, and 1,765 steerage. All this would change with the end of open immigration to the United States in 1924.

The evolution of liner design can be traced through images of four of Holland America Line's six Rotterdams: *the second (1886), top; the fourth (1908), bottom left; the fifth (1959), on pages 20–21; and the sixth (1997), bottom right.*

On the Bridge

A ship's engines are sometimes called its heart and the navigation bridge its head. Always located high and forward for the best visibility, the bridge is manned by the ship's "deck" officers. These officers, the captain and mates, are responsible for navigation and maintenance of the ship. The first, second, and third officers (or mates) take charge of the bridge in a series of "watches" around the clock. The captain will join them on the bridge at all critical times: docking or undocking, in fog, or when a harbor pilot, who provides local navigational expertise, is on board. The engine department is under the control of the chief engineer, supported by a staff similar to the captain's. Today on cruise ships, the hotel department is headed by a hotel manager.

Life on the bridge has changed dramatically since the early days of the liners, when the lookout in the "crow's nest" was an important navigational aid. Knowing its own location always was essential for a ship, and this was once accomplished using an instrument called a sextant to measure the angle of elevation of sun, moon, planet, or certain stars over the horizon. "Sun sights," as they were called, were taken at noon. Using navigational tables, officers could plot the ship's position on a "chart," essentially a maritime map. The Global Positioning System has eliminated the need for these sights. Today, electronic charts are automatically maintained, but most ships keep paper charts as well.

Some important navigational advances are nearly a century old. Radio, first called "wireless telegraphy," was developed in England by Guglielmo Marconi, an Italian, at the beginning of the twentieth century. This was the trans-

Brass fittings abound on the old-fashioned bridge of the SS Independence.

mission of Morse code, dots and dashes, rather than voice. After the *Titanic* sent its SOS, wireless became widely known. Another instrument, the electric-powered, fast-spinning gyrocompass, showed "true" rather than magnetic north.

World War I hastened the development of sonar, which stands for "sound navigation ranging." Sonar sends sound waves underwater, then records them when they bounce back from the bottom or an object. That object could be a submarine, which explains sonar's importance in wartime.

Similarly, the development of radar, which uses radio waves to locate objects above the water, was hastened by World War II. Today, radar is linked to an automatic identification system. An officer can "click" on a ship on a radar screen and learn its name, speed, course (exactly what direction it's going), registration, and more.

Two

The "Atlantic Ferry" and Other Liners

O F ALL THE ROUTES PLIED BY OCEAN LINERS, none was more important than the "Atlantic Ferry"—the collection of ships from many companies and many countries that shuttled between North American ports, New York City primarily, and European: Southampton and Liverpool in England, Le Havre and Cherbourg in France, Hamburg and Bremerhaven in Germany, Rotterdam in Holland, Gothenburg in Sweden, Oslo in Norway, Genoa in Italy, and others. By 1900, these ships were growing in size, speed, and luxury, a trend that would continue through the middle of the twentieth century.

Of course, shipping was by no means limited to the North Atlantic. Liners served all the continents. Many of these routes radiated from Great Britain, since in the early years of the great liners the British Empire was uniquely powerful and extensive. The Peninsular and Oriental Steam Navigation Company, usually called P&O, served India and Australia. The Union-Castle Line offered weekly "mail boat" service to Cape Town in South Africa. From the West Coast of the United States, the Matson Lines and American President Lines reached Hawaii and Asia, and these are just a few examples of the shipping network that linked all the major ports of all the continents.

◀ *Holland America Line's* Rotterdam V *sails down the Hudson River at dusk. Purists were shocked by the ship's nontraditional funnels. However, they admired the liner's "sheer"— the upward sweep of hull at bow and stern that modern cruise ships lack.*

The Ladies' Tea Room aboard Holland America's 1906 Nieuw Amsterdam *offered a cozy shoreside atmosphere, with fireplace, wood accents, and elegant upholstery.*

But the biggest, fastest, and fanciest ships crossed the North Atlantic. Compared with the trek from Great Britain to Australia, South Africa, or India, the distance from Europe to North America was short. The North Atlantic is the most dangerous of oceans, which added to the mystique. Its liners had to be seaworthy enough to cross it in all kinds of weather and all seasons, since, until the 1960s, ships were essential transportation for business and diplomacy as well as pleasure. That was the case all around the world, but nowhere else did so many shipping companies compete as on the North Atlantic.

Liners as National Symbols

"Ships of state," these liners became objects of fierce national pride. Many received government subsidies. In the years leading up to the two world wars, the competition between the merchant navies of England and Germany was nearly as fierce as the military navies' rivalry would be in wartime. These two countries each had two powerful shipping lines, until, in both cases, they merged in the 1930s.

Ships' funnels, or smokestacks, have always had a symbolic

Interiors from late in the era of the liners: stateroom and lounge (top) aboard the Norway, *built in 1962 as the* France, *and dining room aboard the* Rotterdam V.

function as well as their practical one of exhausting smoke and gases from the engine room. The earliest of the great liners had four funnels. Sometimes, however, the fourth funnel was a dummy, placed there just for effect. That was the case with the *Titanic*. In the 1930s, many of the premier ships, such as Holland America's *Nieuw Amsterdam* and Cunard's *Queen Elizabeth*, had two funnels (though the *Queen Mary* had three, as did French Line's *Normandie*). Styles had changed. When the *Ile de France* emerged rebuilt after World War II, its three funnels had been replaced by two. Then Holland America's *Rotterdam* appeared in 1959. Traditionalists were stunned by its two narrow, side-by-side stacks—not proper funnels at all.

Styles of decor changed, too, though it was always opulent.

For all its pleasures, liner travel was transportation, not a joyride, and for many passengers the wild ocean was less than delightful. Seasickness was an ever-present possibility, and rough seas could be frightening. Thus an environment similar to what passengers knew on land could be reassuring. At the turn of the twentieth century, liners' public rooms were wood-paneled, looking as if they might belong in a grand hotel or a fine country home.

Perhaps the most notable liner interiors came in the 1920s, beginning with such ships as the French Line's *Ile de France* and culminating with its fleet mate, the *Normandie*, in 1935. This style was Art Deco, which defined glamour in architecture, transportation, and design for decades. It was modern, sleek, and streamlined, perfect for the speedy liners of the time.

Ships' officers have traditionally been a welcome presence in lounges and dining rooms, as here in the Chart Room aboard the Queen Mary 2. *In the days of line voyages, all senior officers would typically host tables throughout a voyage. In the cruise era, the captain presides at a welcome party and is an occasional host in the dining room.*

The Britanis *was a liner with a long life. It was retired from cruise service in 1994 at the age of sixty-two. The ship was built as Matson Line's* Monterey *for voyages from San Francisco to Hawaii and Australia.*

The Liners Go to War

Twice in the twentieth century, world wars have interrupted the development of the ocean liners, destroyed many of the most beautiful among them, and caused others to change ownership as war "reparations," or compensation paid by the losing side in a war. After World War I, for instance, the Hamburg-Amerika Line's *Imperator* became Cunard's *Berengaria* and its *Vaterland* became United States Lines' *Leviathan*. After World War II, North German Lloyd's *Europa* became the French Line's *Liberté*.

Other ships were lost outright. None was more lamented than the *Lusitania*, torpedoed by a German submarine at the onset of World War I, killing 1,198. The *Normandie* burned and capsized in New York Harbor while being converted for use as a troop ship in World War II. In both wars, virtually all liners served either as troop carriers, often wearing camouflage paint, or hospital ships, their hulls clearly marked with huge red crosses.

After World War II, the liners entered their last great years. Veteran ships returned to peacetime service, and new ones were built.

The Titanic and Other Maritime Disasters

If the *Titanic* had not struck an iceberg in the North Atlantic just before midnight on April 14, 1912, and sunk in two hours and forty minutes with great loss of life, we would know the ship simply as one of a dozen great and luxurious liners that crossed the Atlantic in the years leading up to World War I. Instead, that most storied of all maritime disasters has made the *Titanic* the most famous of ships. Its saga has gripped the public imagination right up to today. This fame has been helped by *A Night to Remember*, a best-selling book by Walter Lord published in 1955; the discovery of the wreck in 1985 and subsequent dives to it; and the 1997 movie *Titanic*, which set box-office records.

Officially named the RMS (for "Royal Mail Steamship") *Titanic,* this White Star Line vessel was the most opulent and largest ship of its time. Said to be unsinkable, it nevertheless sank on its maiden voyage, with a passenger list full of the rich and famous. It had far too few lifeboats for all the passengers and crew aboard—collectively called "souls" on shipboard—and not all were launched. A far higher percentage

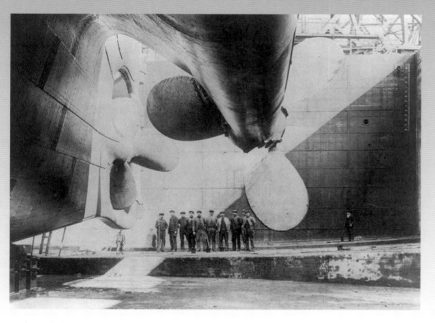

A few of the army of men who worked to build the Titanic *at the Harland and Wolff shipyard in Belfast, Ireland, in the early 1900s pose by its giant propellers.*

of third-class passengers died than did first-class, and the total loss of life was 1,503. The *Titanic* remains the largest ship ever lost in peacetime, with the most casualties. Its sinking resulted in significant changes in maritime law.

Icebergs are dramatic and frightening, but other hazards have posed an even greater threat to shipping—though with global warming, more icebergs are breaking free into the oceans today than ever before. Fire has always been a great concern, and ships have long had sophisticated systems for detecting and extinguishing it. Still, a number of liners have burned and sunk, even into the modern era, including the *Prinsendam* and *Achille Lauro*. Perhaps most dramatic of all was the *Morro Castle*, which sailed between New York and Havana, Cuba. In September 1934, the ship caught fire off the coast of New Jersey, close enough that some passengers swam to shore. One hundred eighty crew and passengers died, partly because only eight of the ship's twelve lifeboats could be launched

Despite sophisticated charts and sonar, groundings are still a risk. So are collisions, particularly in fog. In May 1914, just two years after the *Titanic*'s sinking, a Norwegian coal ship rammed Canadian Pacific's *Empress of Scotland* in heavy fog on the St. Lawrence River in Canada. Mortally damaged, the *Empress* sank in fourteen minutes, taking with it 1,106 souls. Though somewhat less deadly than the *Titanic* tragedy, this sinking has been virtually forgotten—probably because the ship and its passengers were far less grand than the *Titanic* and its wealthy, noted clientele.

Radar might have prevented this collision, but that technology lay well in the future. However, the Swedish America Line's *Stockholm* had radar operating on its bridge in July of 1956 when it rammed the *Andrea Doria*. The flagship of the Italian Line, the *Andrea Doria* was also equipped with the most up-to-date instruments. With its bow totally destroyed, the *Stockholm* limped into New York Harbor. Extensively rebuilt, it was still sailing as cruise ship *Athena* in 2008 at age sixty. The *Andrea Doria* sank, however, a victim of human error on the bridges of both ships.

Spectators gathered on the beach at Asbury Park, New Jersey, to gawk at the burned-out Morro Castle *after it drifted ashore.*

North German Lloyd's SS Bremen *won the Blue Riband in 1929.*

Speeding Across the Atlantic

In the era of transatlantic shipping, unlike in the cruise world of today, speed counted. The informal but much coveted recognition of this speed was the Blue Riband (or "Ribbon"), belonging to the ship making the fastest crossing from Europe to North America. The Blue Riband has always been an unofficial honor, with no committees, judges, or officials bestowing it. The beginning and ending points have varied, so the determination was speed in "knots," the number of nautical miles traveled in an hour.

A nautical mile—basically, one minute of one degree of latitude at the equator—is slightly longer than a "statute," or land, mile.

Speed had its drawbacks, and not all steamship companies made it a top priority. It was expensive, it could cause the ship to vibrate uncomfortably, and it could sometimes be accomplished only by compromising on luxury.

Holland America Line, never awarded the Blue Riband, became known as "The Spotless Fleet," originally because of the high quality of the line's steerage accommodation. The French Line expressed no interest in speed and the Blue Riband, preferring to emphasize luxury and the superb meals for which it was particularly famous. Still, when the French Line's *Normandie*, probably the most admired liner of all time, set the speed record in 1935, the ship steamed into port adorned with a hundred-foot-long blue pennant. By that time there was a physical award to honor the fastest ship: the Hales Trophy, three feet tall and made of silver and gold, given in 1933 by Harold K. Hales, a member of the British parliament. Britain's White Star Line, operator of the *Titanic*, also stressed luxury over speed, as did Germany's Hamburg-Amerika.

That left Cunard Line (with its *Lusitania*, *Mauretania*, and later *Queen Mary*) and North German Lloyd with the *Kaiser Wilhelm Roman II* and sisters *Bremen* and *Europa* to claim, lose, and reclaim the Blue Riband. An Italian Line ship, the *Rex*, also held the title briefly. The *Queen Mary* made the crossing in under four days, at a speed of 30 knots. Its Cunard predecessor, *Britannia*, often considered the first Blue Riband ship, could travel 10.6 knots roughly a century earlier.

But the fastest liner was yet to come: the *United States*, the ultimate speedster, which took the Blue Riband in 1952 with an astounding speed of 35.59 knots. It had been a century since an American ship had held the speed record. This graceful liner was heavily subsidized by the government, which had in mind its wartime potential. The ship's actual top speed was, and remains, a state secret, though the vessel today lies rusting on the Delaware River in Philadelphia. The *Queen Mary* has met a better fate, surviving as a hotel in Long Beach, California.

Cunard White Star's Queen Mary *(top) held the Blue Riband twice, losing it finally to the United States Lines'* SS United States *(bottom).*

Three

The Cruise Era Begins

Cᴀɴᴀᴅɪᴀɴ Pᴀᴄɪꜰɪᴄ ᴏɴᴄᴇ ᴡᴀs ᴀᴍᴏɴɢ ᴛʜᴇ ᴡᴏʀʟᴅ's greatest transportation systems, operating trains, airplanes, hotels, and ships. Its Empress liners crossed both the Atlantic and the Pacific oceans. Its smaller Princess ships sailed the coastal waters from Vancouver in British Columbia. Coincidently, the two giants of the modern cruise industry, which has thrived since the beginning of the 1970s, both got their start with Canadian Pacific ships. The two companies are Carnival, which today has twenty-two ships, and Princess, which has seventeen. These lines and others—Costa, Celebrity, Royal Caribbean, Norwegian Cruise Line (known as NCL), Cunard, and Holland America—offer hundreds of ships that sail all around the world.

◀ *The Twin Towers of the World Trade Center still punctuated the skyline of lower Manhattan when Celebrity Cruises' Horizon sailed in 1991. Since security concerns have outlawed bon voyage parties, well-wishers sometimes try from shore to get the attention of sailing friends and relatives to say farewell.*

Carnival's Festivale *(left) and Chandris's* The Victoria *(right) both began life as Union-Castle Line ships.*

Actually, cruising is nothing new. More than a century ago, ships built to make point-to-point trips would cruise in winter, when demand for transportation on their regular routes was low. The alternative, putting ships into lay-up (out of service), was uneconomical. For instance, Holland America's *Rotterdam* II offered the line's first cruise in 1895. Typically, these pleasure cruises would take passengers to warm places. The Caribbean was and remains a favored cruise destination. Virtually all the great liners assumed the role of cruise ships in the off-season, though they were not ideally designed to do so.

From Crossing to Cruising

Some ships from late in the transatlantic era were built for both crossing and cruising. Companies needed to convert these ships easily from two-class service, when crossing the Atlantic, to single-class, which was usual for cruising. No ship was more cleverly designed to make this conversion than Holland America Line's *Rotterdam* V. Built in 1959, it served as the company's flagship for nearly forty years. The ship made glamorous "world cruises" that lasted for months.

In Skagway, Alaska, the image of Canadian Pacific's Princess Patricia *is reflected in the window of a White Pass & Yukon train.*

Many ocean liners found new careers in cruising, usually with new companies and under new names. One of these was Canadian Pacific's *Empress of Canada*. It was sold to now-giant Carnival Cruise Lines in 1972, becoming the company's first ship, the *Mardi Gras*. This was followed by *Empress of Britain*, which joined the Carnival fleet as the *Carnivale* in 1976. Carnival Cruises would grow and grow, becoming a parent company to much of the cruise industry today.

Union-Castle Line operated from Great Britain to Africa until 1977, outlasting most transatlantic service. Its *Transvaal* *Castle* became the *Festivale*, Carnival's third ship. *Kenya Castle* became the *Amerikanis* and *Dunnottar Castle* became *The Victoria*, both sailing for Chandris, a Greek shipping company that evolved into today's Celebrity Cruises.

A Second Life for the France

Among the most successful liner-to-cruiser makeovers was French Line's *France* to Norwegian Caribbean Line's *Norway*.

The SS Norway *sails past New York's Empire State Building.*

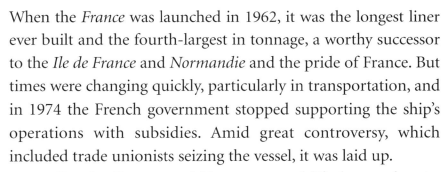

Among the first ships intended specifically for cruising were the Southward, *built in 1971 (top right); the* Westward, *built as the* Royal Viking Star *in 1972 (bottom right); and the* Song of Norway, *built in 1971 (top left).*

When the *France* was launched in 1962, it was the longest liner ever built and the fourth-largest in tonnage, a worthy successor to the *Ile de France* and *Normandie* and the pride of France. But times were changing quickly, particularly in transportation, and in 1974 the French government stopped supporting the ship's operations with subsidies. Amid great controversy, which included trade unionists seizing the vessel, it was laid up.

But the *France* would have a second life, longer than its first, beginning in 1980 as the cruise ship *Norway*. Since speed wasn't essential in cruising, NCL removed one boiler to make the ship less expensive to operate. Large "tenders"—shuttle boats—were carried on the liner's forward deck, so passengers could be quickly transported to shore and back at ports where the ship couldn't dock. Eventually a deck was added to accommodate more passengers.

The *Norway* was the largest cruise ship to have begun life as a liner. Among the smallest was Canadian Pacific's *Princess*

Patricia, which originally served the "Triangle Route" linking Vancouver and Victoria in British Columbia, Canada, with Seattle, Washington. Later, it made summer cruises to Alaska, also for Canadian Pacific. In 1965, during the winter off-season, a U.S. company chartered the ship for cruises to Mexico. The firm liked the "Princess" name, and one of today's giant cruise lines was born.

Four

Modern Cruising

IN THE LAST YEARS OF THE TWENTIETH CENTURY and early in the twenty-first, cruising has boomed. In the 1980s, some forty new cruise ships were launched. In the 1990s came eighty more, then one hundred more in the years 2000 through 2007. Not only are there many, but most are huge. Royal Caribbean's *Freedom of the Seas*—1,112 feet long, with fifteen decks for 4,375 passengers—took over the title of world's largest passenger ship in 2006. It was joined by *Liberty of the Seas* in 2007 and *Independence of the Seas* in 2008. These ships surpass the *Queen Mary 2*, which held the "world's largest" distinction for two years.

Various ways exist to measure the size of a ship. One is length. Another is the number of passengers accommodated, though this can be misleading, since a century ago many ships carried hundreds, even thousands, of steerage passengers in a small space. The best yardstick is

◀ *A Holland America Line ship is followed into St. Thomas by a Royal Caribbean vessel.*

At dusk, Queen Mary 2 *passengers gaze at the* Carnival Spirit *and, in the distance, the* European Vision.

A New Look for Ships

"tonnage"—in particular, "gross register tonnage." This is not a measure of weight, as the name might suggest, but usable interior space. In 1901, the 20,904-ton *Celtic* carried 2,857 passengers, but 2,350 of them were in steerage. At 160,000 tons, *Freedom of the Seas* is almost eight times larger but carries fewer than twice the number of passengers. In part, that's because *Freedom* has an ice-skating rink, a rock-climbing wall, a surfing pool with simulated waves, plus much else that wasn't available even to *Celtic's* first-class passengers, let alone those in steerage.

Contemporary cruise ships look hugely different from ocean liners. Much lower and sleeker, the liners had large open decks fore and aft. These decks were needed to give access to the "holds," where liners carried cargo—which might have included passengers' automobiles and extra luggage. Many trunks and suitcases were tagged "Not Wanted on Voyage" and placed in the hold, to be returned to the passengers on the pier at the end of the voyage. Since a cruise ship carries no cargo, its superstructure can extend much farther forward and all the way aft.

The changed function of the ships also has affected ship design. Liners needed to cross all the oceans at all times and keep to a schedule. This required deep, rugged hulls that could pound safely through rough seas. On the other hand, cruise ships sail mostly on calm seas, rarely venturing onto the North Atlantic in winter, so they can have hulls of shallower "draft" (the depth of a vessel's keel below the water line) and be built taller.

Passenger demand for small private decks—called verandas or balconies—attached to their staterooms has also dramatically altered the look of ships. Seen from the side, ships appear more like apartment buildings than old-fashioned liners. And

The Star Princess *makes good use of every bit of space at its stern.*

"supersizing" has clearly been the trend, with most major cruise lines building ships that dwarf those of even two decades ago. When the *Queen Elizabeth 2* sailed on its maiden voyage in 1969, it was in gross register tonnage the fifth-largest ship ever, surpassed only by its two predecessor *Queens* and the *Normandie* and the *France*. When the *QE2* was retired at the end of 2008, there were more than ninety larger cruise ships afloat.

Propulsion Changes

The way ships are powered has changed enormously. Steam machinery—"reciprocating" engines, with pistons moving up and down in cylinders to turn side-wheels or propeller shafts—replaced sails. Later these engines were replaced by more efficient steam "turbines." In this case, rotor blades spun by steam generated the power. As early as the 1920s, some "motorships" were propelled by diesels. Modern cruise ships use more efficient versions of this type of propulsion.

Despite the example of Brunel's *Great Britain* (see page 15), paddle-wheelers prevailed into the 1860s, though they performed poorly in high seas. When ships rolled, one paddle wheel would lift entirely out of the water, and waves could even smash the wheels. The last paddle-wheeler to hold the transatlantic speed record was the *Scotia*, in 1862. Propellers took over—one, two, or as many as four. On most cruise ships of the twenty-first century, these have been replaced by Azipods, propulsion units that hang below the hull, similar to the way an outboard motor does. They pull rather than push the ship through the water and can move the stern in any direction.

Cunard Line's *Queen Mary 2*, the last true liner built, is among the ships powered by Azipods. The *QM2* is unique among modern ships: it is designed to safely cross the Atlantic, the fiercest of oceans, in all seasons and weather. For two years after its maiden voyage in January 2004, the ship was the world's largest. As the last remnant of the "Atlantic Ferry," it keeps a great tradition alive.

The Queen Mary 2 *is big in every way, from its soaring Britannia Restaurant to its wide teak deck lined with wooden deck chairs.*

At 70,327 gross register tons (GRT), the Queen Elizabeth 2—*once a giant among liners—is dwarfed by Cunard Line fleet mate* Queen Mary 2 *at 148,528 GRT.*

Five

Life on Board

SHIPBOARD LIFE HAS ALWAYS HELD A KIND OF MAGIC. Its nature has changed dramatically over the last hundred years, however, as passenger ships' primary purpose shifted from transportation to pleasure. For passengers traveling in the "cabin" classes—first, second (sometimes called simply "cabin class"), or even third cabin—rather than steerage, the practical need for transportation has always been mixed with enjoyment. Cunard Line's famous slogan, aimed particularly at vacationers, summed it up: "Getting there is half the fun." On the other hand, for the millions of immigrants who had traveled in steerage in the liners' early years, fun was not part of the equation.

Changes in shipboard activities have reflected broader changes in the way we live and what we choose to do for recreation. A century ago, music, dancing, and simple deck sports were the main entertainment a first-class passenger could expect. There might be "fancy-dress balls," for which passengers would make their own costumes, or passenger talent shows. At sea as well as on land, people provided their own amusements.

◀ *Oceania Cruises' Regatta is typical of cruise ships in offering outdoor spaces to swim, soak, read, relax, and walk.*

Today, ships offer elaborate shows aspiring to Las Vegas and Broadway quality, shopping worthy of a mall, and an endless variety of things to do. Physical activities have always been important. Unlike on today's cruises, line-voyage passengers traveled for a week at a stretch or even much longer. The traditional liners had small, simple gymnasiums with rowing machines and stationary bicycles. Now, ships' fitness centers have weights, treadmills, and all the equipment found in a health club.

Ships' libraries today offer computers as well as books.

Walking, Swimming, and Playing

Walking was and is a favorite shipboard ritual. Virtually every liner had a promenade, or walking, deck. Today, there are jogging tracks, basketball courts, climbing walls, and tennis courts. Shipboard tennis is now played using conventional racquets, with netting to prevent the balls from flying overboard. Years ago, passengers enjoyed a game called "deck tennis." It was played on an open court, smaller than used for tennis on land. Instead of using a racquet and ball, players would throw a ring made of rubber or rope across the net. Opponets tried to catch it before it landed.

On the liners, swimming pools were inside and down low, beneath the cabin decks, where there was little motion so water was less likely to slosh out. Today's cruise ships have multiple pools, high up and outdoors. This is possible because the ships typically sail on calm seas in sunny places.

Cruise ships are famous for the amount of food they offer, and meals have always been a highlight of a day at sea.

Afternoon teatime remains an occasion of traditional elegance on many cruise ships.

Harbor pilots are required to accompany ships when they enter or leave port. For some passengers, it's a ritual to be on deck to spot the approaching pilot boat and watch the pilot scramble up a rope ladder to board.

ship's dining rooms, different ones for each class. Passengers sat at assigned tables, the same throughout the voyage, and were served by the same stewards. (All the service staff—whether in the stateroom, dining room, lounges, or on deck—were called stewards, a term still in general use today.) The captain and other senior officers generally hosted tables. Though assigned tables remain the norm for dinner on most cruise ships, options for the other meals (and sometimes even dinner, too) are a growing trend.

On cruises, of course, tours of the ports are a major passenger activity. In addition, the printed daily program is a long list of onboard activities, designed for all ages and all interests. And passengers still do things on their own as well.

Deck Chairs and Steamer Rugs

On the chilly North Atlantic, deck chairs and heavy blankets known as steamer rugs were an important part of a journey. Aboard the liners, passengers rented deck chairs for the voyage. Those chairs were theirs, had their names on them, and would be set in place each morning by the deck steward. On cruises today, deck chairs are free and unreserved, but for many passengers, sitting on deck reading, perhaps a book from an onboard library, remains among the best shipboard experiences.

In the days of the liners, festivities began even before departure with bon voyage parties, lavish send-offs for which guests would come aboard to share champagne with the lucky travelers. Congratulatory telegrams and bon voyage gifts arrived at the staterooms. "All ashore that's going ashore!" would blare over the public address system, and excitement would build. Passengers hurled streamers from the decks while guests did the same from the pier. With two blasts of its throaty whistle, the liner would slip away from the dock, escorted by tugboats.

Another voyage had begun.

Deck tennis and shuffleboard, walking, and reading have long been favored shipboard activities.

Glossary

Atlantic Ferry: Frequent ocean-liner service across the North Atlantic Ocean offered by the shipping companies of many countries.

Bulkhead: Upright partition dividing a ship into compartments to prevent the spread of water or fire.

Cabin class: At first, shipboard accommodation in private rooms rather than the dormitory style of steerage; later, on some ships, a class lower than first and higher than tourist.

Crow's nest: A lookout platform located high on a ship's forward mast.

Draft: The depth of a ship's hull below the waterline.

Dry dock: A basin from which the water can be emptied, used for building a ship or repairing its hull below the waterline.

Finger pier: A dock projecting from the shore.

Flagship: In passenger shipping, a line's most prestigious ship; in the navy, a fleet commander's vessel, which would fly his flag.

Funnel: A ship's smokestack.

Gross register tonnage: A measure of usable interior shipboard space that is the most common yardstick of size; also called "gross tonnage."

High seas: Open waters of an ocean, beyond the control of any country.

Knots: A measure of speed, specifically the number of nautical miles traveled in an hour.

Lay-up: Long-term docking of a ship, either for repairs or because of lack of business.

Line voyage: Point-to-point trip made on a regular basis.

Liner: A ship, especially one carrying passengers on a regular route.

Maiden voyage: A ship's first trip with passengers.

Nautical mile: One minute of one degree of latitude at the equator, slightly longer than a "statute," or land, mile.

Pilot: A local navigational expert who comes aboard to advise the ship's captain in hazardous or congested situations, particularly harbors.

Promenade deck: A deck for walking, typically open. Liners designed for the North Atlantic often had both open and enclosed promenade decks.

Radar: A system using radio waves to identify the location of objects.

Reciprocating engine: The earliest steam propulsion for ships, with pistons that move in and out of vertical cylinders to generate power.

Scuttle: To intentionally sink a ship by breaking a hole in its hull.

Sextant: A navigational instrument used for measuring the altitude of the sun or stars from the horizon to determine a ship's location.

Sonar: A system using reflected underwater sound waves to locate submerged objects or measure the distance to the sea bottom.

Stateroom: A bedroom on a ship, also called a cabin.

Steamer rug: Warm, heavy blanket used by a passenger while sitting in a deck chair.

Steerage: The portion of a ship, originally near the rudder, that provided the cheapest passenger accommodations.

Steward: A shipboard attendant in the dining room, lounge, or cabin, or on deck.

Tender: A boat that shuttles between a ship and the shore at a port where the ship is unable to dock.

The engine room aboard the SS Independence.

Index

Holland America Line